Other titles in the series:
The Crazy World of Aerobics (Bill Stott)
The Crazy World of Cats (Bill Stott)
The Crazy World of Cricket (Bill Stott)
The Crazy World of Golf (Mike Scott)
The Crazy World of the Greens (Barry Knowles)
The Crazy World of the Handyman (Roland Fiddy)
The Crazy World of Hospitals (Bill Stott)
The Crazy World of Housework (Bill Stott)
The Crazy World of Learning to Drive (Bill Stott)
The Crazy World of Love (Roland Fiddy)
The Crazy World of Marriage (Bill Stott)
The Crazy World of the Office (Bill Stott)
The Crazy World of Photography (Bill Stott)
The Crazy World of Rugby (Bill Stott)
The Crazy World of Sailing (Peter Rigby)
The Crazy World of Sex (David Pye)

This paperback edition published simultaneously in 1992 by Exley
Publications Ltd. in Great Britain, and Exley Giftbooks in the USA.
First hardback edition published in Great Britain in 1987 by Exley
Publications Ltd.

Reprinted 1992 and 1993

Copyright © Bill Stott, 1987

ISBN 1-85015-355-8

Printed in Spain by Grafo S.A., Bilbao.

Exley Publications Ltd, 16 Chalk Hill, Watford, Herts WD1 4BN,
United Kingdom.
Exley Giftbooks, 359 East Main Street, Suite 3D, Mount Kisco,
NY 10549, USA.

the CRAZY world of GARDENING

Cartoons by Bill Stott

EXLEY

MT. KISCO, NEW YORK • WATFORD, UK

"OK you bugs and beetles, weeds and weevils, remember me from last year? Well, I'm back!"

"Grandma's been stung again, Daddy..."

"You chauvinist fork!!"

"See what I mean? You don't just switch these on you know…"

"And do you have to do that even when the fuel switch is off?"

"I merely remarked that we hadn't had a bite all day and he took off like a scalded cat!"

"See? I told you that scarecrow wasn't macho enough!"

"When your mother remodels the garden, she doesn't
mess around!"

"If Newton had sat under you, we'd still be waiting for the Theory of Gravity!"

"I don't care where you've come from. You've scorched my lawn!"

"*I always thought this sort of thing only happened in cartoons…*"

"Buy a goat to keep the grass down? Don't be ridiculous! What's that smell...?"

"One of these days I'm going to buy an extension cable and find out how much land I really have..."

"Steve reckons there's this one particular slug..."

"No. I think it was better where we had it in the first place…"

"*Quick! Turn off the water and bring me a knife!*"

"You've decided to tackle the old vegetable patch then?"

"So I said to George, 'We've got the land, we've got the money – let's have a __real__ rock garden!"

"No, wait. Let him get a good blaze going before you ring
the fire department..."

"Ah, here it is… 'Sometimes called Throttleweed from the legend of it being responsible for the disappearance of at least one of Henry VIII's gardeners…'"

"And that's where I fell off the steps..."

*"That's just typical – he's gone fishing and she's home
with the kids!"*

"Would it hurt so much to clean the bathroom when you've finished?"

"*Working hard, my foot! He's been having a smoke behind the shed!*"

"I take it back! I take it back! Your fingers are greener than mine..."

"... and technically speaking, it's yours!"

"I'm signing him on for Pyromaniacs Anonymous next week…"

"That's Mrs Fisher. She has a sticking throttle…"

"I suppose you don't have a deodorized version, do you?"

"You let him go in there __alone__?!?"

"And your little friends dropped by to help you clean out the shed, did they? How nice!"

"Hello dear! Cousin George dropped by; he's out on the lawn practising his chip shots..."

"Hi sweetheart, I'm home early. Come and meet our new
Head of Sales..."

"I'm worried about your dad. He's always talked *to* his plants, but just recently he's started to listen *to* them as well!"

"It <u>is</u> the cat! About 10 minutes ago I spilled some of this new fertilizer on it…"

"David can get very emotional when he's thinning out the raspberry canes..."

"What do you mean WE called the twins Rosemary and Daisy after what we grew together? If we'd called them after what you'd grown, it would be 'Bored' and 'Blistered'!"

"OK, here they come. You wriggle around, and I'll run
up his leg…"

"So it's true! They _can_ read!!"

"Honey? Have you seen my blue pin-stripe suit – the one you don't like...?"

"It's a tribute to my husband's contribution to this garden..."

"Buzz off!"

"There now – be brave! Real gardeners don't cry when they stick the pitchfork through their foot…"

"I didn't have the heart to tell him face to face..."

"I've been reconsidering. Don't you think pools are getting rather common? Why don't we have a nice rock garden instead?"

"I still think you'd get a better spread with a fork!"

"Let's see the Jones's beat that!"

"No this is 28 Fairdrive Hill. You want 28 Fairhill Drive..."

"Bearing in mind the widely-held theory that plants respond and flourish when praised, I'm off to insult a few weeds..."

"Daddy's found a big worm? Well, good for him!"

"No, we can't have a fire. You have to <u>grow</u> something before you can have a fire!"

"Evicting him seems a little heartless. After all, you only discovered him because you decided to clean up this section."

"Dandelion colony, bearing 020, behind the hollyhocks..."

"It's a new rose I've developed. It needs a lot of propping up;
I'm thinking of naming it after you."

"*We're not speaking. I inadvertently disturbed the gerbil's last resting place while planting out the lettuce!*"

*"Strange how the mere mention of trimming the hedge gives
your back spasms..."*

"The lucky horseshoe fell off the garage wall onto my head. I staggered forward, put the mower into 'drive' inadvertently, thereby destroying the fence. Then it overheated, burst into flames, and really ruined my day!"

"C'mon son, don't be chicken! I bet I can dig up more seedlings than you can before he spots us..."

"I still say we're in trouble if the animal protection people find out..."

"I don't seem to be able to switch it off..."

"That's funny. There's a sand wedge and two old putters missing..."

"That's weird. I moved my chair and the hose-pipe dried up…"

"*She hates killing things. She thinks there's a slim chance of insulting the slugs out of the garden.*"

"Why not eat all of one *leaf,* instead of nibbling them all?"

"Stop moaning Gloria! I'm not paying good money for a
summerhouse and then not use it!"

"It's not an unexploded bomb; it's an unexploded gas main!"

"What do you expect from a seed called 'Pot Luck'?"

"Of course, the pressure needs a little fine-tuning..."

"You're quite right Sir! It doesn't say anything about having to wear gloves..."

"For heaven's sake, Norman – it's only a mower!"

"Yes, those little blue berries are poisonous!"

"Wouldn't it be easier just to learn their names?"

Books in the "Crazy World" series
($4.99 £2.99 paperback)

The Crazy World of Aerobics (Bill Stott)
The Crazy World of Cats (Bill Stott)
The Crazy World of Cricket (Bill Stott)
The Crazy World of Gardening (Bill Stott)
The Crazy World of Golf (Mike Scott)
The Crazy World of the Greens (Barry Knowles)
The Crazy World of The Handyman (Roland Fiddy)
The Crazy World of Hospitals (Bill Stott)
The Crazy World of Housework (Bill Stott)
The Crazy World of Learning (Bill Stott)
The Crazy World of Love (Roland Fiddy)
The Crazy World of Marriage (Bill Stott)
The Crazy World of The Office (Bill Stott)
The Crazy World of Photography (Bill Stott)
The Crazy World of Rugby (Bill Stott)
The Crazy World of Sailing (Peter Rigby)
The Crazy World of Sex (David Pye)

Books in the "Mini Joke Book" series
($6.99 £3.99 hardback)

These attractive 64 page mini joke books are illustrated throughout by Bill Stott.

A Binge of Diet Jokes
A Bouquet of Wedding Jokes
A Feast of After Dinner Jokes
A Knockout of Sports Jokes
A Portfolio of Business Jokes
A Round of Golf Jokes
A Romp of Naughty Jokes
A Spread of Over-40s Jokes
A Tankful of Motoring Jokes

Books in the "Fanatics" series
($4.99 £2.99 paperback)

The **Fanatic's Guides** are perfect presents for everyone with a hobby that has got out of hand. Eighty pages of hilarious black and white cartoons by Roland Fiddy.

The Fanatic's Guide to the Bed
The Fanatic's Guide to Cats
The Fanatic's Guide to Computers
The Fanatic's Guide to Dads
The Fanatic's Guide to Diets
The Fanatic's Guide to Dogs
The Fanatic's Guide to Husbands
The Fanatic's Guide to Money
The Fanatic's Guide to Sex
The Fanatic's Guide to Skiing

Books in the "Victim's Guide" series
($4.99 £2.99 paperback)

Award winning cartoonist Roland Fiddy sees the funny side to life's phobias, nightmares and catastrophes.

The Victim's Guide to the Dentist
The Victim's Guide to the Doctor
The Victim's Guide to Middle Age

Great Britain: Order these super books from your local bookseller or from Exley Publications Ltd, 16 Chalk Hill, Watford, Herts WD1 4BN. (Please send £1.30 to cover postage and packing on 1 book, £2.60 on 2 or more books.)